SPIRALIZE!

SPIRALIZE!

40 nutritious recipes to transform the way you eat

Stephanie Jeffs

Interlink Books

An imprint of Interlink Publishing Group, Inc.
Northampton, Massachusetts

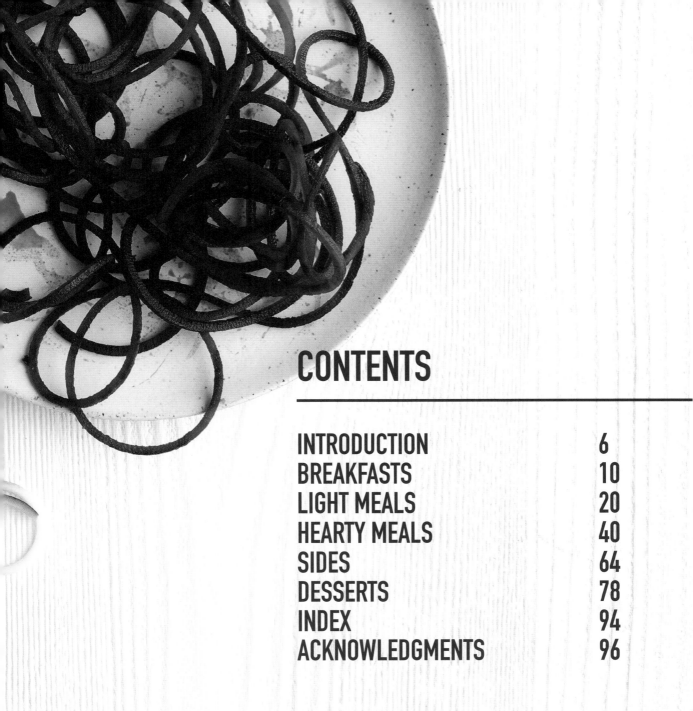

CONTENTS

INTRODUCTION TO SPIRALIZING

We should all try to include more vegetables in our diet, but with so many delicious alternatives on offer it's too easy to give in to the food that we crave rather than what's best for our bodies and, in particular, our waistlines. Having a healthy relationship with food should never mean denying ourselves enjoyment from the meals that we eat. But making small changes to our diet and incorporating more of the food that truly nourishes our bodies is something that can be easily achieved with the help of one simple tool: a spiralizer.

Spiralizing is a delicious alternative to making traditional noodles, pasta, and rice—all of which are laden with refined carbohydrates. Swapping your carbs for veggies—with simply a few cranks of the spiralizer's handle—is a quick and easy way to transform your meals into fiber-packed, low-calorie feasts without sacrificing flavor.

Spiralized vegetables have a similar texture and consistency to pasta and noodles, so you can still enjoy your favorite plate of spaghetti but with only a fraction of the calories and with the added benefits of them being completely raw, vegan, and gluten-free. Spiralizing is also a great way to introduce more vegetables into your child's diet, plus they'll love watching the vegetables being transformed into beautiful ribbons in the blink of an eye.

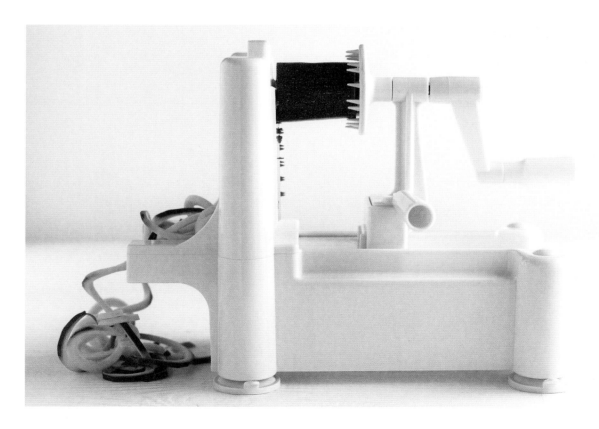

WHICH SPIRALIZER?

To make delicious noodles and spiral pastas, you will need a spiralizer. There are several options currently on the market including handheld, upright, and horizontal machines that are all relatively inexpensive. You can also get attachments for some food processors that have a spiralizing tool. For the recipes in this book, I have used a horizontal spiralizer with three blades. Different brands will have slightly differing noodle sizes but most spiralizers will come with the three blades illustrated below:

Blade 1: fine noodles (or vermicelli style)
Blade 2: medium noodles (or spaghetti/udon style)
Blade 3: ribbon noodles (or tagliatelle style)

The upright spiralizer: the main benefit of an upright spiralizer is that there is no waste (except for the trimmed ends of your fruit/veggies), though it can be tricky to spiralize longer, thinner fruits/veggies. The spiralizing motion is downwards. These are slightly larger machines that suit a larger kitchen.

The horizontal spiralizer: the main benefit of a horizontal spiralizer is that it is easier to store and therefore more practical for most kitchens. The one downside is that there is more potential waste: the inner core of the fruit/vegetable does not get spiralized and a small sausage-shaped stick is left. Even so, these are great chopped into salads, so they needn't be wasted.

The handheld spiralizer: these look like large pencil sharpeners and are perfect for those who have very little storage space. They are very cheap and can be a great way to take your first step into spiralizing. However, they can rely on a lot of hand strength and you will quickly tire, so are best for occasional use.

Food processor attachments: some food processors have a spiralizer attachment. These are great if you have already invested in an expensive processor and want to extend its functionality. Look for attachments that give you the three blade options described here if you can.

A vegetable peeler: though not specifically a sprializer, you can make gorgeous ribbon pasta noodles with most household vegetable peelers. This method takes a little more time and you won't be able to control the length or thickness of the noodles, but it is a great way to get started.

Blade 1

Blade 2

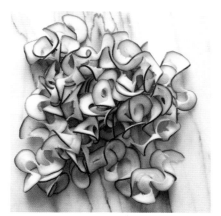
Blade 3

WHAT TO SPIRALIZE?

Not everything can be spiralized—although it can be fun trying! You are looking for fruits and vegetables that meet the following criteria:

– No wider than 4 in/10 cm as this will make it hard to turn the handle.

– No thinner than 1½ in/4 cm as the spiralizer will not be able to make long noodles.

– Solid and without seeds. For example, you can spiralize the top half of a butternut squash but not the bottom half that contains the seeds.

– Fruit and vegetables should be firm. Overripe fruit and vegetables will turn to mush in your spiralizer.

– Not too long. If your veggies are too long they can slip out of the machine or become unmanageable. Cut down long vegetables into shorter lengths before attempting to spiralize.

– Straight. It is very difficult to successfully spiralize a curved vegetable. Use the straightest examples that you can find.

HOW TO SPIRALIZE

Follow the manufacturer's instructions for your spiralizer, but here are a few tips to help you get started:

– Choose firm, straight vegetables.

– Trim your veggies to fit the spiralizer, if necessary. You may need to shorten it or reduce its width (e.g. celery root and turnips that are very round may need reducing slightly).

– You get the best results when you trim the ends of the fruit/veggies for balance (but not always, e.g. apples). When trimming the ends, ensure they are parallel.

– Make sure you choose the right blade for the noodle you are looking for.

– Secure the blade carefully and please be cautious when fitting, removing, and cleaning blades—they are very sharp!

– Fit veggies onto the round holder (usually a metal ring) in the very center or as you turn the handle, the vegetable could fall out; plus your noodles will be very short.

– Secure the veggie with the other end that has spokes (fitted to the handle).

– Choose firm, straight vegetables.

– To spiralize, push the vegetable into the blade and turn the handle as per your spiralizer instructions.

– As you turn the handle, look to see if you are getting the results you had planned: if done well you should be able to spiralize most things into one very long noodle.

– If your noodles are coming out too short (rings or slices), remove the vegetable and try cleaning the blade. Trim the end to create a flat end again, return the veggie to the central ring, and start again.

– The handle should be relatively easy to push and turn: if it is difficult, check the spiralizer to see if there is anything blocking the blade.

ABOUT THE RECIPES

This book is the ultimate beginners' guide to spiralizing, featuring over 40 stylish, creative, and exciting recipes for super-healthy, flavor-packed spiralized meals.

The recipes in this book are all vegan, with a mixture of cooked and raw foods that focus on plant-based, clean eating using quality cold-pressed oils and ethically sourced, healthy, locally produced ingredients. The less we cook food, the more dietary enzymes we get into our systems (which is incredibly important for long-term health, digestion, and the assimilation of nutrients). Spiralizing vegetables and fruits really helps to increase our enzyme intake.

Most of the recipes are portioned to serve one person. To make the recipes for larger groups, simply multiply the volume of ingredients by that number. There are some exceptions to this and some recipes, like the cheesecake (see page 82), are designed for sharing. Every recipe features a full nutritional breakdown to help make clean eating even easier.

BREAKFASTS

Eating a nutritious breakfast is a great way to kick-start your metabolism and power yourself through until lunch, without succumbing to the 11 am munchies. The recipes in this chapter can be put together in a matter of moments and are all designed to give you the best possible start to the day.

APPLE STRUDEL SMOOTHIE BOWL

Preparation time: 10 minutes,
plus soaking
Cooking time: none

Serves 1

1 oz/25 g raisins
1 oz/25 g golden raisins
1 tsp ground cinnamon
1 tsp ground nutmeg
1 large eating apple
1 banana
1 tbsp smooth peanut butter
1 tbsp pumpkin seeds
1 tsp cacao nibs

This is an amazing breakfast, scented with cinnamon and guaranteed to keep your energy levels high until lunch. Plus, if you remember to soak your noodles the night before, it takes only moments to throw together. Left overnight, the apple noodles and dried fruit will plump up and take on the delicious, spicy flavors of a classic apple strudel, despite containing no dairy or processed sugar. The perfect start to the day.

The evening before serving, place the dried fruit in a medium serving bowl and pour in $1\frac{1}{4}$ cups/300 ml water. Sift in the spices and stir to combine, ensuring that the spices are well incorporated and not floating on the surface.

Peel and spiralize the apple using blade 2 (medium, see page 7). Transfer the apple noodles to the bowl and stir to combine. The noodles should sit below the surface of the water, so add more water if needed.

Cover the bowl and transfer to the fridge overnight. Peel the banana and place in the freezer.

The next morning, remove the banana from the freezer and place in a blender. Add $\frac{2}{3}$ cup/150 ml water and the peanut butter. Blend until the mixture is smooth, lump-free, and resembles milk, adding more water if necessary.

Remove the bowl of apple noodles from the fridge—the dried fruit will have bloated and the water will be brown and syrupy. Pour the banana milk over the mixture and stir to combine. Scatter over the pumpkin seeds and cacao nibs, and serve.

NUTRITION (PER SERVING): 532 calories | 13 g protein | 19 g fat (of which 5 g saturates) | 74 g carbohydrate (of which 69 g sugars) | 6 g fiber | 0.2 g salt

CINNAMON NOODLES WITH YOGURT

Preparation time: 5 minutes, plus soaking
Cooking time: none

Serves 1

1 large eating apple
2 tbsp goji berries
1 tsp ground cinnamon
1 tbsp mixed seeds (I used pumpkin, sesame, and sunflower)
yogurt, to serve

Another super-simple recipe that, with a little forward planning, can be thrown together in a matter of moments. Here, delicious apple noodles are combined with vitamin-packed goji berries, nutritious seeds, and a generous dollop of yogurt to ensure that you start the day the right way.

The evening before serving, spiralize the apple using blade 1 or 2 (fine or medium, see page 7), then transfer to a medium serving bowl. Add the goji berries and sift in the cinnamon. Add just enough water to submerge the noodles, cover the bowl, and transfer to the fridge overnight.

The next day, sprinkle the mixed seeds over the top and serve with your choice of yogurt.

NUTRITION (PER SERVING): 247 calories | 7 g protein | 9 g fat (of which 1 g saturates) | 31 g carbohydrate (of which 27 g sugars) | 7 g fiber | 0 g salt

COCONUT OATS WITH FRUITY NOODLES

Preparation time: 10 minutes, plus soaking
Cooking time: none

Serves 1

1 large handful spinach leaves
1 banana, peeled and frozen
scant 2 cups/450 ml low-fat coconut milk
1/3 cup/1 oz/30 g gluten-free oats
2 tbsp chia seeds
1 sharon fruit or persimmon
1 pear
1/2 mango, peeled and chopped

This is the perfect recipe for making at home and then transporting to work for a delicious "al desko" breakfast. Nutritious, delicious, and packed with the flavors of the tropics, daydream yourself somewhere considerably more exotic before tackling the morning emails. Don't be afraid of the spinach; you can't taste it and it is packed full of the nutrients that your body craves.

The evening before serving, place the spinach, banana, and coconut milk in a blender and blend until smooth. Transfer the mixture to a bowl and stir in the oats and chia seeds to combine well. Cover, transfer to the fridge, and leave overnight so the flavors develop and the oats soften.

The next morning, spiralize the sharon fruit or persimmon and the pear using blade 2 (medium, see page 7). Remove the oats from the fridge, then layer the oats, noodles, and chopped mango in a bowl to serve.

NUTRITION (PER SERVING): 702 calories | 14 g protein | 26 g fat (of which 13 g saturates) | 91 g carbohydrate (of which 64 g sugars) | 23 g fiber | 0.1 g salt

BAKED BANANA AND STEAMED APPLE NOODLES

Preparation time: 10 minutes
Cooking time: 20 minutes

Serves 1

1 ripe banana, peeled
4 soft medjool dates, stoned
1 large eating apple

Warm and satisfying, this is the perfect breakfast for cold winter days when there's a nip in the air and you long for nothing more than to stay under the covers. The dates bring a delicious caramel sweetness to the dish but are also packed with fiber that will be sure to keep the mid-morning munchies at bay.

Preheat the oven to 325°F/170°C.

Place the banana, dates, and 1 cup/250 ml water in a blender and blend until smooth.

Spiralize the apple using blade 2 (medium, see page 7), then transfer to a medium baking dish. Pour in the banana and date mixture and ensure that the noodles are evenly covered.

Transfer to the oven and bake for 20 minutes. Transfer to a serving bowl and serve hot.

NUTRITION (PER SERVING): 256 calories | 3 g protein | 0.5 g fat (of which 0.1 g saturates) | 57 g carbohydrate (of which 55 g sugars) | 6 g fiber | 0 g salt

SWEET POTATO WAFFLES WITH MAPLE SYRUP

Preparation time: 15 minutes
Cooking time: 10 minutes

Serves 1

1 sweet potato, peeled
1 tsp ground cinnamon
coconut oil, warmed to a liquid, to grease
1 banana, sliced, to serve
coconut yogurt, to serve
maple syrup, to serve

Though high in natural sugars, maple syrup is packed with manganese, zinc, and calcium, so is a great way to succumb to your sweet tooth while also nourishing your body. Here, it is drizzled over a crispy, cinnamon-scented waffle formed from sweet potato noodles. If you don't own a waffle iron or electric waffle maker, you can still achieve great results by forming the waffle with your hands and frying until browned on both sides.

Preheat your waffle iron on the stove top, or plug in your electric waffle maker to warm.

Spiralize the sweet potato using blade 1 (fine, see page 7). Transfer the noodles to a large bowl and sift over the cinnamon. Pour a generous 2 cups/500 ml boiling water over the noodles and set aside for 5 minutes to soften, cool, and absorb the flavor of the cinnamon. Drain the noodles and use your hands to squeeze out as much water as possible.

Brush the insides of the waffle maker with a thin coating of coconut oil and spread the noodles evenly over the surface. Close the lid and cook until crispy and golden on both sides.

Transfer the waffle to a plate and serve with sliced banana, a dollop of coconut yogurt, and a drizzle of maple syrup.

NUTRITION (PER SERVING, WITHOUT MAPLE SYRUP): 336 calories | 4 g protein | 1 g fat (of which 0.3 g saturates) | 73 g carbohydrate (of which 34 g sugars) | 10 g fiber | 0.3 g salt

LIGHT MEALS

There's more to lunch than a hastily assembled sandwich and a bag of chips. The recipes in this chapter are all light, healthy, and delicious, and can easily be enjoyed at home or "al desko." The perfect way to perk yourself up from the midday slump.

SUPERFOOD SALAD ON A BED OF SOFT NOODLES

Preparation time: 10 minutes
Cooking time: none

Serves 1

1 zucchini
1 tsp olive oil
1 clove garlic, finely chopped
1 tsp maple syrup
3 Brussels sprouts, finely chopped
3 walnuts, coarsely chopped
4 sundried tomatoes, rinsed and chopped
1 handful watercress
1 handful spinach leaves
1 tsp mixed seeds
juice of ½ lime

This colorful salad is packed with enzyme-rich ingredients that check all the nutritional boxes. Spiralizing is a great way of getting more vegetables, like zucchini, into your diet, and by eating them raw, your body will receive 100 percent of their health-giving benefits.

Spiralize the zucchini on blade 3 (ribbon, see page 7), then place in a serving bowl. Drizzle with the olive oil and toss the noodles to coat.

In another bowl, combine the garlic, maple syrup, Brussels sprouts, walnuts, sundried tomatoes, watercress, and spinach, and toss to mix. Place the salad on top of the noodles and scatter on the seeds. Squeeze in the lime juice and serve immediately.

NUTRITION (PER SERVING): 330 calories | 11 g protein | 25 g fat (of which 3 g saturates) | 11 g carbohydrate (of which 9 g sugars) | 9 g fiber | 0.1 g salt

GREEN SUMMER SALAD WITH CUCUMBER NOODLES

Preparation time: 5 minutes
Cooking time: none

Serves 1

1 cucumber
juice of 1 lemon
1 handful watercress
1 handful chard leaves
$1/2$ cup/$2^1/2$ oz/75 g raw peas
$1/2$ cup/$2^1/2$ oz/75 g green beans, sliced lengthways
1 handful fresh mint leaves, finely chopped
1 avocado, peeled and sliced
1 pinch Himalayan salt

This refreshing salad is a detox in a bowl, so perfect for a Monday lunch after an indulgent weekend (let's not pretend we're virtuous all of the time!). Peas are loaded with protein, fiber, and micronutrients, which are anti-inflammatory and help to regulate blood sugars. Mint is great for adding flavor and also has one of the highest antioxidant capacities of any food, plus it aids digestion. Feel free to substitute the leaves to reflect seasonal or local availability.

Spiralize the cucumber using blade 2 (medium, see page 7), then transfer to a serving bowl. Squeeze the lemon juice over the noodles and toss to combine.

Add the watercress, chard, peas, beans, and mint to the bowl and toss everything together.

Serve the salad topped with sliced avocado and a sprinkling of Himalayan salt.

NUTRITION (PER SERVING): 426 calories | 13 g protein | 30 g fat (of which 7 g saturates) | 18 g carbohydrate (of which 7 g sugars) | 16 g fiber | 0.2 g salt

TOASTED PUMPKIN SEED AND ZUCCHINI SALAD

Preparation time: 10 minutes
Cooking time: 8 minutes
Serves 1

1/2 cup/21/2 oz/70 g pumpkin seeds
drizzle olive oil
1 zucchini
1 green tea bag
1 tomato, chopped
1/2 green bell pepper, chopped
1/2 cucumber, chopped
1 pinch Himalayan salt
1 lemon wedge, to serve

This is another light and easy-to-prepare dish that is both delicious and satisfying. The pumpkin seeds give this hot salad its chewiness, nutty taste, and phenomenal health benefits. They are tiny nutritional powerhouses that also house essential plant-based omega-3 fats. This dish will give you half the recommended daily amount of magnesium, which is great for heart health. The addition of soaking your noodles in tea creates a subtle shift to the flavor of this hot salad.

Preheat the oven to 400°F/200°C.

Toss the pumpkin seeds in a drizzle of olive oil and spread on a baking sheet. Place in the oven and cook for 8 minutes, or until lightly toasted.

Spiralize the zucchini using blade 2 (medium, see page 7), then transfer to a large bowl. Add the green tea bag and pour in enough boiling water to cover. Set aside for 3–5 minutes to allow the noodles to soften and infuse with the tea.

Drain the noodles, discarding the tea bag, and squeeze out any excess water by hand. Transfer the noodles to a serving dish, along with the remaining ingredients and the pumpkin seeds.

Toss everything together and serve with a wedge of lemon alongside.

NUTRITION (PER SERVING): 508 calories | 24 g protein | 36 g fat (of which 6 g saturates) | 18 g carbohydrate (of which 8 g sugars) | 10 g fiber | 0.1 g salt

CRUNCHY SALAD WITH STICKY MANGO SAUCE

Preparation time: 10 minutes
Cooking time: none

Serves 1

1 mango, peeled and diced
1 cup/250 ml pineapple juice, freshly squeezed
1 pinch chili flakes
1 tsp fresh root ginger, finely chopped
1 tsp sesame oil
1/2 celery root, peeled
1/2 cucumber
1 thick broccoli stem
2 tbsp mixed seeds
1 handful cilantro, chopped

This salad has a fiery bite to it, which is great if, like me, you love spicy food. If you're chili-phobic, manage the amount of spice to your own taste and, likewise, don't be afraid to load it up if you like it hot! The sauce makes enough for two or three salads, so it's perfect for keeping in the fridge and will last for up to 4 days.

Place the mango, pineapple juice, chili flakes, ginger, and sesame oil in a blender and blend until smooth. Set aside.

Spiralize the celery root and cucumber using blade 2 (medium, see page 7), then transfer to a serving bowl. Pour the mango sauce over the noodles.

Spiralize the broccoli stem using blade 1 (fine, see page 7).

Scatter the seeds over the salad and top with the broccoli spirals and the chopped cilantro.

NUTRITION (PER SERVING): 487 calories | 14 g protein | 19 g fat (of which 3 g saturates) | 56 g carbohydrate (of which 50 g sugars) | 18 g fiber | 0.4 g salt

SWEET POTATO RÖSTI

Preparation time: 10 minutes
Cooking time: 35 minutes

Serves 1

½ sweet potato, peeled
1 small onion, finely chopped
scant ½ cup /100 ml low-fat coconut milk
1 tbsp coconut flour
1 pinch Himalayan salt
1 handful fresh parsley, chopped
1 handful spinach leaves
1 scallion, finely sliced
lemon wedge

This is a twist on the traditional Swedish dish, made with sweet potato for a less starchy result and a vibrant hit of color. Potato doesn't always have to be naughty, and sweet potatoes are higher in digestion-aiding fiber and vitamin A than the regular kind. This rösti has a crunchy, golden shell and is al dente on the inside—steamed and softened but not soggy. To achieve this, it is important not to lay your rösti out too flat on the baking tray: give it some depth and flip it halfway through cooking. This is a nice big, burly plate of food for when it's cold outside and you want something warm in your belly.

Preheat the oven to 325°F/170°C.

Spiralize the sweet potato using blade 1 (fine, see page 7), then place in a bowl with the onion.

Blend the coconut milk, flour, and salt to make a sticky batter. Pour the batter over the sweet potato and combine to make sure everything is well coated.

Line a baking sheet with parchment paper and turn out the mixture on to the sheet. Using your hands, form the rösti into a thick round, around 6 in/15 cm in diameter. Using a wooden spatula, neaten the sides of the rösti (any pieces that are sticking out will quickly burn).

Transfer to the oven and bake for 15 minutes. Remove from the oven and flip over with a large wide spatula, reshaping the rösti if necessary. Return to the oven for a further 15-20 minutes, until golden and crispy.

Transfer the rösti to a serving plate and garnish with freshly chopped parsley. Serve alongside a salad of spinach leaves and scallions, and a wedge of lemon.

NUTRITION (PER SERVING): 327 calories | 7 g protein | 11 g fat (of which 7 g saturates) | 43 g carbohydrate (of which 15 g sugars) | 13 g fiber | 1.2 g salt

HOT GREEN TEA NOODLE SALAD

Preparation time: 15 minutes
Cooking time: 20 minutes

Serves 1

For the dressing:
1/2 cup/125 ml sesame oil
2 tbsp tamari soy sauce
1 tbsp maple syrup
1 clove garlic, finely chopped
1/2 red chili, finely chopped
1/2 green chili, finely chopped
juice of 2 lemons
3/4 in/2 cm fresh ginger, finely sliced
1/2 scallion, finely sliced

For the salad:
1 red bell pepper
1/2 onion, quartered
1/2 head broccoli, chopped
1/2 sweet potato, peeled and chopped
2 tbsp coconut oil, warmed to a liquid
1 celery root
1 green tea bag

This hot vegetable salad is dressed in a fiery sauce that can be made ahead and used at a moment's notice. You can adapt this recipe to use up any vegetables that you have left in the bottom of your fridge, but do give the celery root noodles a try as they impart a subtle celery flavor to the dish that is perfectly complemented by the green tea. As well as tasting great, celery root is a great source of vitamin K, iron, and calcium, plus it is packed with phosphorous, making it a sure-fire way to kick-start your metabolism.

Preheat the oven to 400°F/200°C.

To make the dressing, combine all the ingredients in a lidded jar or beaker and shake vigorously to combine. Set aside until needed.

For the salad, place the red bell pepper, onion, broccoli, and sweet potato in a roasting pan and drizzle with the oil. Toss to coat, then transfer to the oven for 20 minutes, until gently roasted but still retaining some bite.

Spiralize the celery root using blade 2 (medium, see page 7), then transfer to a large bowl. Add the green tea bag and pour in enough boiling water to cover. Set aside for 3-5 minutes to allow the noodles to soften and infuse with the tea.

Drain the noodles, discarding the tea bag, and squeeze out any excess water by hand.

Transfer the noodles to a serving bowl and pour on some of the dressing; this packs a kick, so use moderately. Serve alongside the roasted vegetables. Any leftover dressing can be kept in the fridge for up to 3 days.

NUTRITION (PER SERVING WITH 1 TABLESPOON DRESSING): 630 calories | 14 g protein | 36 g fat (of which 21 g saturates) | 50 g carbohydrate (of which 28 g sugars) | 24 g fiber | 1.2 g salt

RAW CHINESE "STIR-FRY" WITH CRUNCHY NOODLES

Preparation time: 20 minutes, plus soaking
Cooking time: none

Serves 1

For the marinade:
½ cup/125 ml sesame oil
2 tbsp tamari soy sauce
1 tbsp maple syrup
1 clove garlic, finely chopped
½ red chili, finely chopped
½ green chili, finely chopped
juice of 2 lemons
¾ in/2 cm fresh ginger, finely sliced
½ scallion, finely sliced

For the stir fry:
½ large parsnip, peeled
1 cup/3½ oz/100 g mushrooms, finely sliced
3 sugar snap peas, finely sliced
2 baby corns, sliced lengthways
¼ green bell pepper, sliced
¼ small savoy cabbage, finely shredded
1 head broccoli, finely chopped
1 scallion, finely sliced
1 tbsp sesame seeds
½ tsp dried chili flakes
1 tbsp chopped walnuts, to garnish

This dish really benefits from a long marinate in its sticky sauce. Over time, the crunchy vegetables will start to soften and really take on those classic stir-fry flavors. Because this dish is completely raw, none of the health-giving nutrients from the vegetables are lost during its preparation.

To make the marinade, combine all the ingredients in a lidded jar or beaker and shake vigorously to combine. Set aside until needed.

For the stir-fry, spiralize the parsnip using blade 2 (medium, see page 7), then transfer to a large bowl. Add the rest of the stir-fry ingredients to the bowl and pour in the marinade. Using your hands, massage all the ingredients together to coat in the sauce.

Cover the bowl and set aside to marinate for at least 30 minutes, but, for best results, up to 4 hours. Return to the bowl every 30 minutes and give it a shake to ensure that the ingredients get a fresh coating of sauce.

When you are happy with the flavors, lift the stir-fry out of the marinade and transfer to a serving dish. Serve, garnished with chopped walnuts.

NUTRITION (PER SERVING): 981 calories | 31 g protein | 77 g fat (of which 11 g saturates) | 29 g carbohydrate (of which 21 g sugars) | 26 g fiber | 4.2 g salt

CUCUMBER NOODLE SALAD WITH FENNEL, CHARD, AND QUINOA

Preparation time: 10 minutes
Cooking time: 10 minutes

Serves 1

For the dressing:
1 cup/5½ oz/150 g peas
1 large handful spinach leaves
1 bunch mint leaves
3 tbsp apple cider vinegar
3 tbsp olive oil
juice of 1 lime
1 tbsp tamari
1 tsp maple syrup

For the salad:
⅛ cup/1 oz/25 g quinoa
½ cucumber
¼ fennel bulb, finely sliced
3 radishes, finely sliced
1 scallion, finely sliced
2 tbps sesame seeds
1 handful chard leaves

This super-healthy salad is served with a punchy mint and pea dressing that gives the dish a real zing. The addition of protein-packed quinoa to the ingredients gives it real bite and makes it a satisfying and substantial lunch. The recipe for the dressing makes plenty, so keep any leftovers in the fridge and use over the next couple of days.

First prepare the dressing: place all of the ingredients into a blender and blend until smooth. Transfer to the fridge while you make your salad.

Put the quinoa in a bowl and pour in enough cold water to cover. Leave to soak for a couple of minutes, then drain. Put a scant ½ cup/100 ml water in a pan and bring to a boil. Add the quinoa to the pan and cook on a gentle simmer for 10 minutes until it has softened and absorbed the water. Drain the quinoa, if necessary, and set aside to cool.

Spiralize the cucumber using blade 2 (medium, see page 7), then place the noodles in a serving dish. Add the remaining salad ingredients and toss everything together by hand.

Dress the salad with a couple of spoonfuls of the dressing (you will have plenty left over) and scatter on the cooled quinoa. Serve.

NUTRITION (PER SERVING | WITH 2 TABLESPOON DRESSING): 384 calories | 14 g protein | 26 g fat (of which 4 g saturates) | 20 g carbohydrate (of which 6 g sugars) | 8 g fiber | 0.6 g salt

STUFFED CABBAGE ROLLS WITH BUCKWHEAT

Preparation time: 20 minutes
Cooking time: 10 minutes

Serves 2

½ cup/3½ oz/100 g roasted buckwheat

6 cabbage leaves, hard stems removed

½ celery root, peeled

1 tsp olive oil

½ onion, finely chopped

2 cups/7 oz/200 g mushrooms, finely chopped

1 scallion, sliced

1 pinch chili flakes

⅓ bottle gourd or zucchini, peeled

½ organic, low-salt vegetable stock cube

Despite its name, buckwheat isn't actually a grain, but is a member of the rhubarb family and is the perfect gluten-free substitute for rice and processed carbs. It's great for aiding digestion and contains rutin, which is helpful for lowering blood pressure. If you would like to keep this dish completely raw you could use sprouted buckwheat, but for simplicity I have used the roasted variety, which is really easy to prepare.

Put the buckwheat in a bowl, cover with water, and set aside to soak for 5–10 minutes, then drain.

Meanwhile, bring a pan of water to a boil and cook the cabbage leaves for 5 minutes until soft. Drain the leaves, retaining the water, then lay them on clean dish towel to cool.

Spiralize the celery root using blade 2 (medium, see page 7) then transfer the noodles to a food processor. Pulse the noodles until they have reached a rice-like texture.

Heat a wok over medium heat and add the olive oil. Add the onion to the pan, followed by the buckwheat, celery root rice, mushrooms, scallion, and chili flakes. Stir-fry for 5 minutes until all the ingredients are softened, then transfer to a bowl to cool.

Take a spoonful of the mushroom and buckwheat mixture, form into a ball, and place in the center of one of the cabbage leaves. Wrap the cabbage leaf around the ball to form a parcel, securing with a toothpick, if necessary. Repeat with the remaining cabbage leaves.

Spiralize the bottle gourd or zucchini using blade 1 (fine, see page 7) and divide the noodles between two serving bowls. Place three cabbage parcels in the center of each bowl.

Return the reserved cabbage water to the pan and crumble in the stock cube. Bring to a boil and remove from the heat. Ladle the hot broth into the bowls and leave everything to soak for a couple of minutes. Remove any toothpicks from the cabbage balls and serve warm.

NUTRITION (PER SERVING): 286 calories | 11 g protein | 4 g fat (of which 0.4 g saturates) | 48 g carbohydrate (of which 6 g sugars) | 9 g fiber | 0.8 g salt

ASIAN NOODLE SOUP

Preparation time: 20 minutes
Cooking time: none

Serves 1

For the soup:
1 tbsp arame flakes
½ bottle gourd, peeled (radish, daikon radish, or parsnip would also work well)
½ green bell pepper, finely chopped
½ celery stick, finely chopped
2 large choy sum leaves
1 handful kale, stalks removed
1 handful enoki mushrooms
1 tbsp fresh cilantro, chopped, to garnish

For the paste:
1 small red chili, finely chopped
1 small green chili, finely chopped
¾ in/2 cm fresh ginger, finely chopped
1 scallion, finely sliced
1 clove garlic, finely chopped
½ tsp cold-pressed sesame oil
1 tbsp tamari soy sauce
½ tsp onion salt

Bottle gourd (also known as calabash, dudhu, or lauki) brings a delicate perfume and a nice crunch to this piquant dish. Most large supermarkets sell them, but a large radish or parsnip would work just as well. The vegetables in this recipe are simply poached in the broth they are served in, making for a delicious, enzyme-rich soup with a hint of fire. I like to eat this with chopsticks and then slurp the broth straight from the bowl.

Place the arame flakes in a small bowl and cover with boiling water. Set aside to soak for at least 10 minutes, then drain.

Meanwhile, spiralize the bottle gourd using blade 1 (fine, see page 7) and set aside.

Now make the paste. Place the chilies, ginger, scallion, and garlic in the base of a large soup bowl and pour in boiling water to just cover. Set aside for 3 minutes to allow the ingredients to start to sweat and the flavors infuse.

Add the sesame oil, tamari, and onion salt to the soup bowl and give everything a stir to combine into a wet paste, adding a little more boiling water if necessary.

Add the noodles and the remaining soup ingredients to the bowl, finishing with the drained arame. Pour in enough boiling water to cover the ingredients and almost fill the bowl. Use chopsticks to give everything a stir, making sure that the broth paste is well mixed into the liquid.

Set aside for a few minutes to allow the flavors to develop. Serve warm, garnished with fresh cilantro.

NUTRITION (PER SERVING): 76 calories | 4 g protein | 3 g fat (of which 0.5 g saturates) | 6 g carbohydrate (of which 6 g sugars) | 4 g fiber | 4.8 g salt

HEARTY MAINS

There are times when a salad just won't cut it and you want something substantial and warming to fill you up. The dishes in this chapter will curb your cravings, whether for a big pile of pasta, a warming curry, or a slice of pizza, without any need to feel guilty afterwards.

TOMATO PASTA BAKE

Preparation time: 10 minutes
Cooking time: 40 minutes

Serves 2

2 zucchini
3 large tomatoes
6-8 semi-dried apricots
1 tsp garlic granules
1 tsp olive oil

There are few things more comforting than a bowl of steaming pasta dripping with fragrant tomato sauce. This is the perfect dish for when you get the craving for pasta but don't want the carbs or the gluten bloat. I use zucchini a lot because they're great for the waistline, have a high water content, and are loaded with micronutrients, particularly just under the skin (which is why you should never peel them before spiralizing). Cooking the noodles long and low in the sauce will make them tender and full of flavor.

Preheat the oven to 300°F/150°C.

Spiralize the zucchini using blade 2 (medium, see page 7). Transfer the noodles to a medium baking dish and set aside, reserving the zucchini cores.

Place the remaining ingredients, along with the zucchini cores, in a blender and blend until smooth. Pour the sauce over the noodles and mix together to ensure that they are thoroughly coated.

Transfer to the oven and bake for 40 minutes until the noodles are soft and tender. Serve hot.

NUTRITION (PER SERVING): 170 calories | 5 g protein | 3 g fat (of which 0.5 g saturates) | 27 g carbohydrate (of which 27 g sugars) | 8 g fiber | 0.1 g salt

NOODLE PIZZA

Preparation time: 20 minutes, plus soaking
Cooking time: 40 minutes

Serves 6

For the base:

1 cup/7 oz/200 g roasted buckwheat

1/2 cup/2 1/2 oz/70 g sunflower seeds

1/2 cup/2 1/4 oz/60 g milled flax seeds

1/4 cup/1 3/4 oz/50 g flax seeds, soaked for 2 hours

1/3 cup/1 3/4 oz/50 g sundried tomatoes, soaked in water overnight to rehydrate

1 tbsp canola oil

2 cloves garlic

1/4 onion

1 pinch sea salt

For the toppings:

1/2 onion

1/2 pear

1/2 sweet potato, peeled

1 handful spinach leaves

1 cup/250 ml tomato sauce (follow recipe on page 46)

1 handful mushrooms, sliced

1/2 red bell pepper, sliced

1 small handful olives

1 tbsp capers

Everyone's favorite guilty pleasure, here pizza has had a makeover to reinvent it as a protein- and vitamin-packed meal, loaded with super-healthy seeds and vegetables. If you want to make this completely raw, you could use a dehydrator to dry out the base overnight at 100°F/40°C, but cooking it in the oven will give great results and is a lot quicker!

Preheat the oven to 325°F/170°C.

Start by making the base. Place all the ingredients in a food processor along with 3 tbsp water and process to a thick paste. Line a large baking sheet with parchment paper and tip the paste on to the sheet. Using a rubber spatula, spread the paste into a 12-in/30-cm round, about 1/4 in/5 mm thick. Transfer the base to the oven and bake for 20 minutes.

Meanwhile, spiralize the onion, pear, and sweet potato using blade 2 (medium, see page 7) and spread out on a separate baking sheet. Transfer to the oven and bake for 15 minutes. Keep warm until ready to use.

After 20 minutes, remove the pizza base from the oven and cover with another sheet of parchment paper. Place a large plate over the paper and, using an oven glove, invert the pizza base on to the plate. Peel off the original sheet of paper and slide the base back on to the baking sheet. Return to the oven and bake for a further 10 minutes.

Remove the pizza from the oven and cover with the spinach leaves. Spoon on the tomato sauce and add the noodles, along with the remaining toppings.

Return to the oven and bake for a further 10 minutes until crisp and golden. Transfer to a large plate or board and serve hot.

NUTRITION (PER SERVING): 425 calories | 12 g protein | 18 g fat (of which 2 g saturates) | 48 g carbohydrate (of which 13 g sugars) | 11 g fiber | 1.1 g salt

SPAGHETTI WITH VEGGIE BALLS

Preparation time: 20 minutes,
plus soaking
Cooking time: 20 minutes

Serves 2

For the mushroom balls:
2 mushrooms, finely chopped
4 tbsp tamari soy sauce
2 tbsp apple cider vinegar
1 cup/3½ oz/100 g sunflower
seeds, soaked for 2 hours
¼ cup/1¼ oz/35 g walnuts
¼ onion, chopped
½ tsp garlic granules

For the tomato sauce:
½ cup/2¼ oz/60 g sundried
tomatoes, soaked in water
overnight to rehydrate
3 soft medjool dates
1 large salad tomato
1 clove garlic
¼ onion, chopped
1 tsp olive oil
juice of ½ lemon
1 pinch Himalayan salt
1 tbsp mixed Italian herbs

For the spaghetti:
1 zucchini

This vegan, gluten-free version of the classic Italian dish hits all the right flavor notes and is laden with vitamin-packed vegetables. The umami-rich mushroom balls have a great meaty texture and any leftovers make excellent snacks for the lunchbox. The tomato sauce is raw and served at room temperature, meaning that you are getting 100 percent of the possible nourishment from the dish. If you're hankering for the taste of Parmesan, sprinkle with a tablespoon of nutritional yeast flakes before serving.

Preheat the oven to 400°F/200°C.

To make the mushroom balls, place the mushrooms in a bowl with the tamari and cider vinegar. Place the sunflower seeds in a separate bowl and cover with water. Set both bowls aside to soak for 2 hours.

Drain the mushrooms and sunflower seeds, and transfer to a food processor with the walnuts, onion, and garlic granules and pulse to a coarse paste.

Using your hands, shape the mixture into 9 golf ball-sized balls and place on a baking sheet. Transfer to the oven and bake for 20 minutes.

Meanwhile, prepare the sauce. Put all the ingredients in a blender and blend until smooth. Set aside to allow the flavors to develop while the mushroom balls are baking.

Spiralize the zucchini using blade 2 (medium, see page 7) and divide the noodles between two serving plates.

Place three mushrooms balls on each plate of noodles (you will have extras, but they can be stored in the fridge) and spoon over some of the tomato sauce to serve.

NUTRITION (PER SERVING): 420 calories | 13 g protein | 27 g fat (of which 4 g saturates) | 27 g carbohydrate (of which 18 g sugars) | 8 g fiber | 2.1 g salt

RIBBON PASTA WITH CREAMY MUSHROOM SAUCE

Preparation time: 5 minutes, plus soaking
Cooking time: none

Serves 1

For the sauce:
½ cup/125 ml almond milk
½ cup/3 oz/85 g dried porcini mushrooms, rehydrated
1 tbsp olive oil
1 tsp lemon juice
½ teaspoon onion powder
1 clove garlic
1 tbsp cashews, soaked for 2 hours
1 tsp nutritional yeast flakes
1 tsp tamari soy sauce
1 tbsp tahini

For the pasta:
1 daikon radish

The sauce used in this recipe is delicious, versatile, and can be used in any number of dishes. The quantities below will make more sauce than you need, so store the rest in the fridge and use it up over the next couple of days. As with most of the raw food that I prepare, the sauce tastes its best when left to come back to room temperature, rather than eaten straight from the fridge.

Place all the ingredients for the sauce in a blender and blend until smooth and creamy. Set aside.

Spiralize the daikon radish using blade 3 (ribbon, see page 7), then transfer to a serving bowl. Pour over ½ cup/125 ml of the mushroom sauce and serve.

NUTRITION (PER SERVING, USING 125 ML SAUCE): 209 calories | 7 g protein | 18 g fat (of which 3 g saturates) | 5 g carbohydrate (of which 4 g sugars) | 2 g fiber | 1.5 g salt

ZUCCHINI PAPPARDELLE WITH SPINACH

Preparation time: 5 minutes
Cooking time: 5 minutes

Serves 1

6–10 almonds, finely chopped
2 tbsp tamari soy sauce
1 small zucchini
1 tsp sesame oil
1 scallion, sliced
½ sweet green chili, sliced
1 clove garlic
juice 1 lemon
1 handful spinach leaves
1 tsp sesame seeds

This is delicious and light but also hot and filling. Though there's no sauce, the spinach and zucchini expel liquid as they cook, creating a light broth that melds with all the flavors of the dish. Use a big handful of spinach as it tastes great and is full of health-giving vitamins. The almonds make a lovely crunchy garnish but also add an injection of vitamin E, copper, magnesium, and high-quality protein.

Place the almonds and tamari in a small bowl and set aside to soak.

Meanwhile, spiralize the zucchini using blade 2 (medium, see page 7), then set aside.

Heat a wok over a high heat and warm the sesame oil. Add the scallion, chili, and garlic to the pan and stir-fry for 1 minute, keeping everything moving in the pan. Add the lemon juice to the wok and, when it starts to steam, add the spinach. Once the spinach begins to wilt, toss the zucchini noodles into the pan with the sesame seeds and cook for 1 minute more.

Transfer to a serving plate and serve, garnished with the tamari-soaked almonds.

NUTRITION (PER SERVING): 175 calories | 8 g protein | 12 g fat (of which 2 g saturates) |
6 g carbohydrate (of which 6 g sugars) | 3 g fiber | 5.6 g salt

NOODLE BURRITO

Preparation time: 15 minutes
Cooking time: 3 hours

Serves 1-2

For the wrap:
2 zucchini
3 large tomatoes
6 sundried tomatoes, washed
6-8 semi-dried apricots
1 tsp garlic granules
1 tsp olive oil

For the filling:
½ small celery root, peeled
2 tbsp French green (Puy) lentils, cooked
mint leaves, chopped, to garnish

This inside-out burrito features spiralized zucchini actually in the wrap, rather than used as filling. The wrap itself is full of flavor, so I've kept the filling simple. This is a large burrito, so you may want to share it or save half for later, but it's packed with vegetables, fruit, and pulses that are essential for nourishing the body and the soul, so there's absolutely no shame in polishing off the whole thing! Start the cooking ahead, since it needs to be cooked slowly.

Preheat the oven to 225°F/110°C.

Spiralize the zucchini using blade 2 (medium, see page 7), then set aside in a bowl, retaining the zucchini cores.

Place the remaining wrap ingredients, along with the zucchini cores, in a blender and blend until smooth. Pour the purée over the noodles and, using your hands, mix thoroughly to coat.

Line a large baking sheet with parchment paper and tip the noodles onto the sheet. Spread the noodles to make a 12-in/30-cm round. The wrap should be very thin so it can be rolled after cooking. Transfer to the oven and cook with the oven door slightly ajar for 3 hours, flipping the wrap by inverting onto another lined baking sheet halfway through.

When cooked, the wrap should have an almost rubbery consistency that allows it to be rolled without cracking. Overcooking will make it crisp, meaning that it will crack when you try to roll it.

Meanwhile, spiralize the celery root using blade 1 (fine, see page 7), then place the noodles in a food processor. Pulse to create a fine rice, then set aside.

To assemble, lay the wrap out flat and spoon the rice and lentils into the center. Carefully roll the wrap into a tight cylinder and slice in half. Serve garnished with chopped mint leaves.

NUTRITION (PER SERVING): 401 calories | 15 g protein | 9 g fat (of which 1 g saturates) | 54 g carbohydrate (of which 45 g sugars) | 22 g fiber | 1.1 g salt

ASPARAGUS AND BOK CHOY NOODLE BOWL

Preparation time: 10 minutes
Cooking time: 10 minutes

Serves 1

2 cardamom pods
2 black peppercorns
1 pinch cinnamon
2 cloves
$1/2$ celery root, peeled
$1/2$ tsp sesame oil
1 clove garlic, finely chopped
2 stems asparagus, chopped into $3/4$ in/2 cm pieces
1 tsp maple syrup
1 head bok choy
1 tsp sesame seeds
juice of $1/2$ lime

Heralding the start of the warmer months, asparagus season brings with it an inclination to turn your face to the sun and bring some lighter food to the table. This fragrantly spiced dish is half broth, half stir-fry and is packed with some great immune-system boosting vegetables. Asparagus is full of fiber, folic acid, and vitamins A, B, and C, and bok choy, like all cruciferous vegetables, is a brilliant dietary antioxidant.

Crush the cardamom, peppercorns, cinnamon, and cloves to a fine powder with a mortar and pestle, then set aside.

Spiralize the celery root using blade 2 (medium, see page 7) and transfer the noodles to a bowl. Pour boiling water over the noodles to cover and set aside.

Place a wok over high heat and warm the sesame oil. Add the garlic to the pan, followed quickly by the asparagus and the crushed spices. Cook for 2–3 minutes, until the asparagus starts to brown, then add the maple syrup.

Using a pair of tongs, lift the noodles out of the water and into the pan; do not drain the noodles first, since any water clinging to them will create steam and aid the cooking process. Keep everything moving around the wok for another minute, then add the bok choy and another ladleful of water.

Cook for 2 minutes more and then tip the contents of the wok into a serving bowl. Sprinkle with the sesame seeds and squeeze in the lime juice. Serve hot.

NUTRITION (PER SERVING): 141 calories | 6 g protein | 6 g fat (of which 1 g saturates) | 10 g carbohydrate (of which 9 g sugars) | 11 g fiber | 0.3 g salt

HOT PEANUT NOODLE SALAD

Preparation time: 10 minutes
Cooking time: 5 minutes

Serves 1

1 tbsp unroasted peanuts
1 celery root, peeled
1 tbsp olive oil
1 leek, finely sliced
2 scallions, finely sliced
1 tsp maple syrup
1 tbsp crunchy peanut butter
1 pinch chili flakes
2 tbsp coconut milk
1 large lettuce leaf, to serve

This pretty, hot salad is served in a lettuce leaf, which makes the perfect substitute for a starchy, carb-heavy bread or wrap. Peanuts are amazing sources of vitamin E, niacin, and folate, as well as protein and manganese. They are a perfect energy food too, with over 500 calories per 100 g, and are a great source of monounsaturated fatty acids, which is useful for lowering cholesterol.

Preheat the oven to 400°F/200°C.

Spread the peanuts on a baking sheet and toast in the oven for 8 minutes or until lightly golden. Set aside.

Spiralize the celery root using blade 2 (medium, see page 7), then place the noodles in a bowl. Pour in enough boiling water to cover the noodles and leave to soak for 2 minutes. Drain and set aside.

Place a wok over high heat and warm the olive oil. Add the leek and scallions to the pan and keep them moving for a couple of minutes until starting to brown. Add the maple syrup, peanut butter, and chili flakes to the pan, followed by the coconut milk. When the pan has started to steam, add the roasted peanuts and keep moving everything around the wok. Add the celery root noodles and toss to coat in the sauce and combine with the other ingredients. Remove wok from the heat to cool slightly.

Place the lettuce leaf on a serving plate and spoon in the slightly cooled noodles. Serve warm.

NUTRITION (PER SERVING): 539 calories | 18 g protein | 39 g fat (of which 10 g saturates) | 20 g carbohydrate (of which 14 g sugars) | 19 g fiber | 0.8 g salt

THAI RED CURRY WITH NOODLES

Preparation time: 10 minutes
Cooking time: none

Serves 1

½ celery root, peeled

½ cup/2¼ oz/60 g cashew nuts, soaked for 2 hours

1 cup/225 ml low-fat coconut milk

½ onion, finely chopped

3 cherry tomatoes

3 sundried tomatoes, rinsed

juice of ½ lime

½ small red chili, chopped

½ avocado, peeled and pitted

1 tsp fresh root ginger, grated

1 clove garlic

½ tsp ground cumin

½ tsp cayenne pepper

½ tsp paprika

½ tsp turmeric

1 pinch garam masala

cilantro, to garnish

olive oil, to serve

coconut yogurt, to serve

The strength of this curry lies in its aromatic blend of ingredients, which combine to create a delicately spiced and fragrant sauce. The avocado makes the sauce really creamy, while also boosting its nutritional content. If you like, you can add some more vegetables to this to sit in the sauce, but it's already quite rich and is a great companion to the celery root noodles.

Spiralize the celery root using blade 1 (fine, see page 7), then set aside.

To make the sauce, place the cashews and coconut milk into a blender and blend until smooth. Add the remaining ingredients and continue to blend until a smooth, thick paste is formed.

Place the noodles on a serving plate and scatter on the cilantro. Spoon the curry paste over the noodles, or serve in a separate bowl. Drizzle olive oil over the coconut yogurt to serve on the side.

NUTRITION (PER SERVING): 771 calories | 18 g protein | 61 g fat (of which 22 g saturates) | 29 g carbohydrate (of which 16 g sugars) | 17 g fiber | 1.1 g salt

SPICY VEGETABLE STIR-FRY

Preparation time: 10 minutes

Cooking time: 10 minutes

Serves 1

$\frac{1}{3}$ zucchini

$\frac{1}{2}$ onion

$\frac{1}{2}$ apple

1 tbsp olive oil

1 red chili, chopped

1 clove garlic, finely chopped

$\frac{1}{4}$ red bell pepper, sliced

2 mushrooms, sliced

2 baby corns, halved lengthways

4–6 snow or sugar snap peas, halved lengthways

juice of $\frac{1}{2}$ lemon

1 tbsp tamari soy sauce

$\frac{1}{2}$ mango, peeled and chopped

1 handful cilantro, chopped, to serve

A classic vegetable stir-fry is given the spiralizer treatment by substituting the traditional egg noodles with light and healthy fruit and vegetable ones. You can play around with the vegetables that you use in this dish and adjust the level of spice to your taste; the key thing here is that the entire dish, noodles included, is packed with nutritious, body-nourishing vegetables.

Spiralize the zucchini and onion using blade 1 (fine, see page 7), then set aside in separate bowls. Spiralize the apple using blade 2 (medium, see page 7), then set aside.

Heat the oil in a wok over medium heat and add the chili, garlic, and bell pepper. Cook for 1 minute, then add the mushrooms and spiralized onions to the wok. Keep everything moving and cook for 2 minutes until the onions have softened. Add the apple noodles to the pan, along with a splash of water, and cook for a further 2 minutes. Add the baby corn, snow or sugar snap peas, lemon juice, and tamari and cook for 2 minutes more. Add the zucchini noodles to the pan and toss to coat, cook for a final minute, and stir in the mango. Remove from the heat and set aside for 2 minutes while all the flavors infuse.

Transfer the stir-fry to a plate and garnish with cilantro before serving.

NUTRITION (PER SERVING): 338 calories | 7 g protein | 23 g fat (of which 3 g saturates) | 21 g carbohydrate (of which 21 g sugars) | 8 g fiber | 1.9 g salt

WILD MUSHROOM YAKITORI

Preparation time: 10 minutes
Cooking time: 10 minutes

Serves 1

For the mushrooms:
4–6 large wild mushrooms
2 tbsp tamari soy sauce

For the noodles:
½ zucchini
1 green tea bag
⅓ stalk lemongrass, bashed

For the stir-fry:
1 tsp canola oil
1 medium onion, finely chopped
1 scallion, finely sliced
2 cloves garlic, finely chopped
¾ in/2 cm fresh root ginger, finely chopped
1 stalk lemongrass, bashed and finely sliced
½ green bell pepper, finely sliced
1 generous handful beansprouts, washed and patted dry
2–3 tsp tamari soy sauce
1 tsp maple syrup
juice of 1 lime

For this recipe you really have to use wild mushrooms. They are dry, hold much less water, and impart an incredible flavor to the dish. When grilling the mushrooms, you are aiming for a long-roast effect; the tamari should dry out on the mushroom and leave just a hint of flavor. Soaking the noodles in green tea and lemongrass adds a wonderfully subtle perfume that brings the whole dish together. This dish is best if you marinate the mushrooms overnight.

First, place the mushrooms in a bowl and pour in the tamari. Cover and set aside for at least 4 hours, preferably overnight.

After the mushrooms have soaked, thread them lengthways onto a bamboo skewer and set aside. Preheat the grill (or broiler) to medium.

For the noodles, spiralize the zucchini using blade 2 (medium, see page 7) and transfer to a bowl with the green tea bag and lemongrass. Pour in a scant 1 cup/200 ml boiling water and set aside to soak and cool.

Place the mushrooms skewers on the grill (or on a grill pan under the broiler) to cook for about 3 minutes on each side; they burn easily so keep a close eye on them and turn occasionally.

Meanwhile, make the stir-fry. Preheat a wok over a high heat and add the canola oil. Add the onion, scallion, and garlic and toss to combine. Add the ginger and lemongrass to the pan along with a couple of tablespoons of water and keep everything moving around to avoid it burning.

When the vegetables have started to wilt, add the green pepper and beansprouts to the pan, followed by the tamari, maple syrup, and lime juice. Stir to combine, then remove from the heat.

Drain the noodles and transfer to a serving plate. Place the stir-fried vegetables over the noodles and top with the mushroom skewers. Serve hot.

NUTRITION (PER SERVING): 163 calories | 7 g protein | 4 g fat (of which 0.4 g saturates) | 21 g carbohydrate (of which 16 g sugars) | 7 g fiber | 3.7 g salt

THAI COCONUT NOODLE SOUP

Preparation time: 10 minutes
Cooking time: 30 minutes

Serves 2

For the soup:
½ sweet potato, peeled
1 tbsp coconut oil, warmed
to a liquid
½ celery root, peeled
½ onion, finely chopped
1 tsp chili flakes
3 baby corns, chopped
lengthways
scant 1 cup/200 ml
vegetable stock
scant ½ cup/100 ml
coconut milk
juice of ½ lime
1 handful beansprouts
1 handful alfalfa sprouts
1 tbsp toasted coconut flakes

For the broth paste:
1 tsp garlic granules
½ tsp chili flakes
¼ tsp ground cumin
½ red onion, finely chopped
1 scallion, finely chopped
1 lemongrass stalk,
finely chopped
¼ tsp turmeric
1 tsp maple syrup
½ tsp peanut oil
juice of 1 lime

This fragrant soup is full of the flavors of Thailand and makes a great alternative to a heavy, rice-based dish. The sweet potato noodles are baked separately and served submerged in the soup; they add bulk, texture, and a delicious sweetness to the dish that elevates this light-seeming offering into a substantial and satisfying main course.

Preheat the oven to 325°F/170°C.

Spiralize the sweet potato using blade 2 (medium, see page 7), then place on a baking sheet. Drizzle on the coconut oil and bake in the oven for 30 minutes, or until tender.

Meanwhile, make the broth paste by blending all ingredients in a blender, or mashing with a mortar and pestle. Set aside.

Spiralize the celery root using blade 1 (fine, see page 7), then place in a bowl. Pour in boiling water to cover and set aside to soften for 5 minutes. Drain and set aside.

Place a wok over a high heat, then add the soup broth paste and stir until fragrant, then add the onions, followed by the chili flakes, baby corn, vegetable stock, coconut milk, and lime juice. Keep everything moving around the pan and bring the soup to a gentle simmer. Add the celery root noodles and beansprouts to the pan and cook for a further 2 minutes. Remove the wok from the heat and set aside.

Remove the sweet potato noodles from the oven and place in the base of a large serving bowl. Ladle the soup over the sweet potato noodles and top with alfalfa sprouts and coconut flakes. Serve hot.

NUTRITION (PER SERVING): 336 calories | 7 g protein | 20 g fat (of which 15 g saturates) | 29 g carbohydrate (of which 13 g sugars) | 10 g fiber | 1.3 g salt

SIDES

Snacking doesn't have to be a bad thing, and eating little and often will help to keep you healthy and satisfied. The recipes in this chapter can be made ahead and kept on hand for when you feel like a snack.

NOODLEKRAUT

Preparation time: 10 minutes
Cooking time: none

Makes a 1 pint/450 g jar

1 tbsp Himalayan salt
2 cloves garlic, peeled
1 tsp juniper berries
1 tsp allspice berries
1 sprig rosemary
1 sprig dill
2 cucumbers
1 large cabbage leaf

Fermented foods are brilliant for increased gut health and overall wellness. This wonderful noodlekraut not only tastes great but will flood your body with beneficial probiotics—the good bacteria that help to heal the gut. Use this recipe to experiment with other vegetables and styles of noodle. In the picture opposite I have used cucumber and turnip with different spiralizer blades.

Start by making the pickling brine: in a large jug, measure out a generous 2 cups/500 ml water (preferably filtered), add the salt, and stir until dissolved.

Smash the garlic cloves and place in a sterilized 1 pint/450 g pickling jar with the juniper and allspice berries, rosemary, and dill.

Spiralize the cucumbers using blade 2 (medium, see page 7), then press them into the jar, using a wooden spoon to firmly pack them in. Pour in the brine as you go and keep filling the jar with cucumber noodles and brine until full. The noodles should be covered in brine with a gap of around 1 in/2.5 cm at the top of the jar to allow the noodles to expand and ferment. Place the cabbage leaf over the cucumber and press down to ensure that the noodles stay completely submerged in the brine.

Seal the jar and leave in the fridge. Release the lid daily to allow for any gas to escape and replace tightly.

After several days, the noodlekraut will be ready to eat. Once opened, keep in the fridge and consume within 3 weeks.

NUTRITION (PER 1 TABLESPOON [25 G] SERVING): 1 calorie | 0.1 g protein | 0 g fat (of which 0 g saturates) | 0.2 g carbohydrate (of which 0.2 g sugars) | 0.1 g fiber | 0.4 g salt

CRUNCHY BEET AND CARROT NOODLES WITH AVOCADO DIP

Preparation time: 5 minutes
Cooking time: 20 minutes

Serves 1

1 small beet
1 medium carrot
1 tsp coconut oil, warmed until liquid
1 pinch Himalayan salt
1 ripe avocado

These crunchy noodles make the perfect afternoon snack and are a great alternative to starchy fries or chips. The colors here are a real visual feast, but you could experiment with different vegetables depending on what's in season and available locally.

Preheat the oven to 325°F/170°C.

Spiralize the beet and carrot using blade 2 (medium, see page 7). Spread the noodles out on a baking tray and drizzle with the coconut oil. Bake in the oven for 20 minutes, or until crispy and slightly browned.

Scoop the flesh of the avocado into a bowl and mash with a fork. Add a pinch of salt and stir to combine.

Transfer the noodles to a serving plate and serve alongside the dip.

NUTRITION (PER SERVING): 420 calorie | 6 g protein | 32 g fat (of which 9 g saturates) | 21 g carbohydrate (of which 18 g sugars) | 14 g fiber | 2.3 g salt

NOODLE GHANOUSH

Preparation time: 5 minutes
Cooking time: 20 minutes

Serves 1

1 large eggplant
½ zucchini, peeled
2 tbsp tahini
1 tbsp lemon juice
1 clove garlic, finely chopped
1 pinch Himalayan salt
1 tbsp cold-pressed olive oil
1 tsp paprika
orange wedges, to serve

This is my take on the classic Middle Eastern dip, with a noodle twist. The eggplant imparts a delicious smoky flavor that transports you straight to the souk, which can be heightened by toasting the eggplant over an open flame, if you like. The magnesium and fiber-packed zucchini noodles add bulk to the dish, meaning you don't have to serve this with the traditional bread accompaniments.

Preheat the oven to 400°F/200°C.

Prick the eggplant all over with a fork and place on a baking sheet. Bake in the oven until the flesh is soft, at least 15-20 minutes. Scoop the flesh into a colander and set aside to drain for 20 minutes.

Meanwhile, spiralize the zucchini using blade 2 (medium, see page 7), then set aside.

Place the eggplant in a bowl with the tahini, lemon juice, garlic, salt, and olive oil, and mash everything together until smooth. Add the noodles to the bowl and stir to combine.

Sprinkle the paprika over the dish and serve with orange wedges alongside.

Nutrition (per serving): 323 calories | 9 g protein | 27 g fat (of which 4 g saturates) | 7 g carbohydrate (of which 6 g sugars) | 10 g fiber | 2.0 g salt

"CHEESY" FRIES

Preparation time: 10 minutes
Cooking time: 20 minutes

Serves 1

1 baking potato
1 tsp coconut oil, warmed to a liquid
1 tsp nutritional yeast flakes

There are times when it feels like only a plate of fries will do, but this clean tasting alternative is a great, guilt-free way to satiate your carb cravings. Soaking the noodles to remove the starch is vital in achieving a "clean" noodle, so don't be tempted to skip this step. Nutritional yeast flakes may sound weird, but are a great, dairy-free way of achieving the umami-rich flavor that cheese lovers hanker for.

Preheat the oven to 350°F/180°C

Spiralize the potato using blade 2 (medium, see page 7), then place in a bowl. Pour in enough cold water to cover, then set aside to soak for 5 minutes to remove any excess starch. Drain the noodles, squeezing out any excess water with your hands.

Drizzle the coconut oil over a baking sheet and spread the potato noodles over the top, spreading them out to cover the entire sheet.

Bake in the oven until crunchy and golden, about 20 minutes. They burn easily, so check them every few minutes.

Remove from the oven and transfer to a serving plate. Sprinkle with the nutritional yeast flakes, ensuring that everything gets an even covering. Serve hot.

NUTRITION (PER SERVING): 225 calories | 5 g protein | 4 g fat (of which 3 g saturates) | 41 g carbohydrate (of which 1 g sugars) | 4 g fiber | 0 g salt

NOODLE SLAW

Preparation time: 10 minutes
Cooking time: none

Serves 6

½ small pineapple, chopped

1 mango, peeled and pitted

1 cup/7 oz/200 g sunflower seeds, soaked for 2 hours

2 scallions, finely sliced

1 pinch chili flakes

1 carrot

½ apple

1 celery root, peeled

3¼ in/8 cm raw horseradish

1 handful red cabbage leaves, finely chopped

½ onion, finely chopped

This coleslaw is dairy-free, with a sweet and spicy mango and pineapple sauce taking the place of the traditional mayonnaise. It really is worth taking the time to find fresh horseradish for this dish, since it adds a delicious underlying warmth. This makes a great side dish to all kinds of foods and looks beautiful in the center of a table laden with food.

Set aside a handful of pineapple for later and place the rest in a blender. Add the mango, drained sunflower seeds, scallion, and chili flakes and blend until smooth. Set aside.

Spiralize the carrot, apple, and celery root on blade 2 (medium, see page 7), then transfer to a large bowl. Spiralize the horseradish using blade 1 (fine, see page 7) and add to the bowl.

Add the cabbage, onion, and reserved pineapple chunks to the bowl and pour in the sauce. Using your hands, massage all the ingredients together to ensure everything is well coated. Serve.

NUTRITION (PER SERVING): 267 calories | 9 g protein | 16 g fat (of which 2 g saturates) | 17 g carbohydrate (of which 11 g sugars) | 8 g fiber | 0.1 g salt

CILANTRO AND MINT FRESH ROLLS

Preparation time: 10 minutes
Cooking time: none

Serves 1

½ mango, peeled and pitted
1 tbsp lime juice
1 tsp chili flakes
¼ cup/1 oz/30 g raw almonds
1 tsp tamari soy sauce
½ celery root, peeled
1 carrot
¼ cup/1 oz/30 g canned butter beans
3 rice paper sheets
1 sprig fresh mint leaves, chopped
1 sprig fresh cilantro leaves, chopped
1 small red chili, finely chopped

These pretty parcels are a feast for the eyes as well as the taste buds. They are served with a zingy mango sauce that is easy to make but packed with flavor. This recipe is for a single portion of three rolls but, scaled up, these would make a great, super-healthy appetizer for a dinner party.

Place the mango, lime juice, and chili flakes in a blender and blend until smooth. Set aside until needed.

In a food processor, coarsely chop the almonds, then transfer to a bowl. Pour in the tamari and stir to ensure an even coating. Set aside.

Spiralize the celery root and carrot using blade 1 (fine, see page 7), then transfer to separate dishes.

In a bowl, mash the butter beans until smooth using the back of a fork. Add the tamari-soaked almonds and stir to combine.

Prepare a space on your countertop and lay out a clean dish towel. Have your bowls of prepared ingredients close at hand.

Fill a large bowl with boiling water and add the rice sheets. Leave to soften for one minute, ensuring that they do not fold over on themselves (they are very sticky).

Lay the soaked rice papers out flat on the dish towel. Spread a spoonful of the butter bean and almond mixture over each sheet, then top with the noodles, herbs, and chili. Fold each wrap, turn it over on itself once, tuck in the top and bottom edges, then fold over once more to seal. You will need to work quickly since these are very sticky.

Transfer the wraps to a serving plate and serve with the mango dipping sauce.

NUTRITION (PER SERVING): 337 calories | 12 g protein | 18 g fat (of which 2 g saturates) | 26 g carbohydrate (of which 21 g sugars) | 13 g fiber | 1.5 g salt

CALIFORNIA NOODLE ROLLS

Preparation time: 10 minutes
Cooking time: none

**Makes 6 pieces
(or 2 large cones)**

½ cucumber

½ ripe avocado, peeled and pitted

2 tsp curry powder

1 pinch Himalayan salt

2 square nori sheets

½ carrot, cut lengthways into fine sticks

3-4 cherry tomatoes, quartered

2 tsp sesame seeds

1 handful alfalfa or radish sprouts

These make an excellent mid-afternoon snack or can be served with a salad as a light lunch. Though they seem fussy, they are easy to assemble and can even be put together on your desk at work. If the individual rolls seem like too much of a faff, simply form two large cones; the important thing is to load up on those delicious sprouted seeds—nature's finest and most nutritious enzyme-rich food.

Spiralize the cucumber using blade 2 (medium, see page 7), then set aside.

In a bowl, mash the avocado with a fork. Add the curry powder and salt and mix to combine.

Lay your nori sheets out on a flat, clean, dry surface and spread a spoonful of the avocado mixture over the top. Place half the noodles, a few carrot sticks, a few tomato quarters, and 1 tsp of sesame seeds onto each sheet, being careful not to overfill. Top each sheet with half of the alfalfa sprouts.

Carefully roll each nori sheet into a cylinder, packing the filling as tightly as you can (use a sushi mat if you have one, but freehand is fine). Slice each sheet into three equal-size pieces and serve. Alternatively, you can roll each one into a large cone.

NUTRITION (PER PIECE): 61 calories | 3 g protein | 4 g fat (of which 0.7 g saturates) |
2 g carbohydrate (of which 1 g sugars) | 5 g fiber | 0.5 g salt

DESSERTS

Having the occasional something sweet at the end of a meal is a real treat and something to be savored, not to feel guilty about. The recipes in this chapter are free of dairy and refined sugars, but packed with health-giving fruits, nuts, and seeds. There's even a bit of chocolate, which should keep even the most determined sugar fiend happy.

FRUIT NOODLE TRIFLE

Preparation time: 15 minutes,
plus soaking
Cooking time: none

Serves 1

1 tsp chia seeds
1 cup/225 ml mango or
apple juice
½ cup/2¼ oz/60 g cashews
2 tbsp coconut oil, warmed
1 tbsp agave or maple syrup
1 sweet red apple, halved
2 tbsp lemon juice
½ mango, peeled and pitted
1 firm persimmon
1 handful mixed berries (I used
raspberries, blackberries,
blueberries, and strawberries)
½ kiwi, peeled and sliced

For the topping:
1 handful goji berries
1 tsp cacao

This is a simple, light, and refreshing take on a classic British trifle that is packed with fruit and topped with tasty dairy-free cashew custard. You can make this dish your own by experimenting with different types of fruit and making the most of what's in season and abundant. The cashew custard is a great imitation of the real thing, plus it is packed with heart-healthy monounsaturated fats, so I would really recommend giving it a try, though a topping of yogurt would also be healthy and delicious.

Place the chia seeds in the bottom of a glass and cover with the mango or apple juice. Transfer to the fridge and leave for at least 2 hours, preferably overnight, for the seeds to bloat.

Place the cashew nuts and the goji berries for the topping in separate bowls, cover both with water, and set aside for at least 2 hours, then drain.

Place the cashew nuts in a blender with the coconut oil and agave or maple syrup. Blend until smooth and creamy, then set aside.

Using a sharp knife, cut one of the apple halves into thin slices and sprinkle with 1 tablespoon of the lemon juice to prevent them from browning.

Place the mango in a blender and blend until smooth; set aside.

Spiralize the remaining half apple using blade 1 (fine, see page 7), then trim the noodles into 4-in/10-cm lengths with a pair of scissors. Toss the noodles in the remaining lemon juice and set aside.

Spiralize the persimmon using blade 2 (medium, see page 7), then set aside.

When ready to assemble the trifle, remove the glass containing the chia seeds from the fridge. Add a layer of berries to the bottom of glass, pushing them down into the seeds. Now build the trifle by alternating layers of the noodles, blended mango, and sliced apple and kiwi, adding a few goji berries between each layer.

Stop layering once the glass is almost full and spoon a layer of the cashew custard over the fruit. Sprinkle with a few of the goji berries and sift some cacao over the top. Serve.

NUTRITION (PER SERVING): 749 calories | 10 g protein | 39 g fat (of which 22 g saturates) | 83 g carbohydrate (of which 76 g sugars) | 12 g fiber | 0.1 g salt

RAW PERSIMMON AND ORANGE CHEESECAKE

Preparation time: 30 minutes, plus resting
Cooking time: none

Serves 16

For the base:
1 cup/3¹⁄₂ oz/100 g almonds
1 cup/3¹⁄₂ oz/100 g hazelnuts
1¹⁄₄ cups/7 oz/ 200 g semi-dried apricots
2-5 drops orange extract
2 tsp coconut oil, warmed

For the filling:
3 firm persimmons
3 cups/12 oz/350 g raw cashew nuts, soaked for 2 hours
³⁄₄ cup/3¹⁄₂ oz/100 g coconut yogurt
seeds of 1 vanilla pod
1 tsp rose water
juice of ¹⁄₂ lemon, at room temperature
1 tbsp agave nectar
1 tsp ground turmeric
scant ¹⁄₂ cup/5¹⁄₂ oz/150 g coconut oil, warmed to a liquid
juice of ¹⁄₂ orange, at room temperature

For the topping:
1 firm persimmon
1 handful raw coconut flakes
zest of one unwaxed orange

Though most of the recipes in this book are for single portions, this raw "cheesecake" is so good that your friends will be begging you for a slice, despite the fact that it's completely dairy free and contains no refined sugars. Packed with vitality-boosting nuts and fruit, this dessert manages to be creamy, rich, and indulgent while remaining (relatively) virtuous.

First make the base. Place the nuts in a food processer and pulse until coarsely chopped. Add the apricots and continue to process until the mixture resembles couscous; processing the mixture beyond this will release too much oil from the nuts, resulting in a greasy base to your cheesecake. Add the orange extract and coconut oil, process the mixture again for 30 seconds to blend in the oils, then transfer the mixture to the base of a 7-in/18-cm springform pan. Use your hands to firmly pack the base into the bottom of the pan, making sure it is flat and evenly covered. Set aside while you make the filling.

For the filling, spiralize the persimmon using blade 2 (medium, see page 7), then set aside.

Place the remaining filling ingredients, except the orange juice, into a high-powered blender. Blend the mixture, gradually adding the orange juice as you blend. The final mixture should look like a thick pancake batter: if yours is too thick, loosen it with a few drops of warm water (do not use cold water since it will cause the coconut oil to harden).

Spread half of the persimmon noodles over the cheesecake base, making sure they are evenly distributed and not piled in the center. Pour half of the filling over the base, level, then add another layer of noodles. Pour the remaining filling over the top, completely concealing the noodles, and level the surface with a spatula. Transfer the cheesecake to the fridge to set for at least 4 hours. To tell if the cake is set, press very gently on its surface and pull your finger away; if the surface is firm to the touch and your finger comes away clean, then the cake is ready.

Carefully remove the cake from the pan and transfer to a serving plate. Spiralize more persimmon noodles and pile them on the top of the cake to decorate. Sprinkle with the coconut flakes and orange zest and serve, slicing the cake with a cold, sharp knife. The cheesecake will keep for up to five days in the fridge.

NUTRITION (PER SERVING): 362 calories | 8 g protein | 30 g fat (of which 13 g saturates) | 14 g carbohydrate (of which 11 g sugars) | 3 g fiber | 0 g salt

BAKED PEAR WITH BEET NOODLES AND CHOCOLATE SAUCE

Preparation time: 10 minutes
Cooking time: 30 minutes

Serves 1

1 large beet
2 tbsp rose water
1 pear, peeled, stalk intact
2 tbsp maple syrup
juice of 1/2 orange

For the chocolate sauce:
2 tbsp coconut oil, warmed to a liquid
1 tsp cacao powder
1 tsp maple syrup

The earthy flavor of beet is wonderful when paired with dark chocolate, as in this fragrant dessert. The chocolate sauce is made with raw cacao, which is rich in calcium, iron, vitamin C, and magnesium, and, here, is sweetened only with coconut, making it both indulgent and virtuous. The pear adds a lifting hint of sweetness to the rich flavors of this dish and the subtle perfume of the rose water lies at the back of every delicious mouthful. The perfect way to end a meal.

Preheat the oven to 325°F/175°C.

Wash the beet and spiralize using blade 2 (medium, see page 7). Set the noodles on a flat baking sheet, drizzle with the rose water, and set aside.

Cut the base off the pear so that it sits upright on a flat surface. Place the pear in an ovenproof ramekin dish and pour over the maple syrup and orange juice. Transfer to the oven for 10 minutes.

Once the pear has been cooking for 10 minutes, add the beet noodles to the oven and cook both for a further 20 minutes, basting the pear in its juices at 10-minute intervals.

Meanwhile, place the warmed coconut oil, cacao powder, and maple syrup in a small bowl and stir to combine.

Place the noodles on a serving plate and arrange into a nest shape. Sit the pear in the center of the nest and pour any residual juices from the ramekin over the top. Finally, pour the chocolate sauce over the pear and noodles and serve.

Nutrition (per serving): 472 calories | 5 g protein | 23 g fat (of which 19 g saturates) | 56 g carbohydrate (of which 52 g sugars) | 11 g fiber | 0.5 g salt

STICKY DATE AND PECAN NOODLES WITH VEGAN BANANA ICE CREAM

Preparation time: 15 minutes, plus freezing
Cooking time: 25 minutes

Serves 1

1 small butternut squash
3 pitted medjool dates, soaked in water overnight
3 pecans

For the ice cream:
1 banana, peeled and frozen
seeds from 1 vanilla pod

This is a super-simple, super-tasty dessert that is composed of just three ingredients: butternut squash, dates, and pecans. Despite being free of dairy and refined sugars, by some alchemy this dish manages to capture the essence of a classic sticky toffee pudding and remain healthy. During cooking, the date paste drips down through the noodles and caramelizes them as they poach. The dessert is served with a dairy-free banana and vanilla ice cream, which can be made in advance and kept in the freezer.

To make the ice cream, place your frozen banana and vanilla seeds in a high-powered blender and blend until smooth and the consistency of soft-serve ice cream. This can be eaten straight away but, for best results, transfer to the freezer for several hours until solid.

Preheat the oven to 325°F/170°C.

Using a sharp knife, slice the butternut squash in half across its middle. Save the larger, bottom half of the squash for use in another dish and peel the smaller, seedless half. Spiralize the squash using blade 1 (fine, see page 7).

Place the noodles in a small, one-portion ovenproof ramekin and press down to make sure that they are packed in tightly. They will condense and break down during cooking, so don't worry if the ramekin looks overfull.

Reserving the soaking water, drain the dates and transfer them to a food processor. Process until you achieve a smooth, wet, and sticky consistency, adding a bit of the soaking water if needed.

Transfer the date paste to a bowl with the pecans and stir to thoroughly coat the nuts in the paste. Spoon the mixture on top of the noodle-filled ramekin, pressing the mixture to the edges of the dish to seal, and ensuring that the noodles are entirely covered.

Place in the oven and bake for 25 minutes until the paste begins to bubble.

Remove from the oven and set aside to cool for two minutes. Put a serving plate over the top of the ramekin and invert the dessert onto the plate, giving it a gentle shake to release it from the ramekin. Serve hot.

NUTRITION (PER SERVING): 437 calories | 6 g protein | 13 g fat (of which 1 g saturates) | 69 g carbohydrate (of which 54 g sugars) | 9 g fiber | 0 g salt

APPLE RIBBONS DIPPED IN CHOCOLATE

Preparation time: 10 minutes
Cooking time: none

Serves 1

1/2 cup/125 ml coconut oil, warmed until liquid
2 tsp cacao powder
2 tsp agave or maple syrup
2-4 drops of vanilla extract
1 large sweet red apple
1 handful raw peanuts, chopped

This dessert tastes like everyone's favorite coconut chocolate bar and is really fun to make and eat! As with all the chocolate recipes in this book, you don't need to worry about refined sugars, since you can see exactly what's going into it. Not only is this chocolate sauce virtuous, but it also contains coconut oil, which is incredibly good for the skin, helps with weight loss, and contains beneficially saturated fats that help the body feel satiated for longer.

In a small bowl, combine the coconut oil, cacao powder, agave syrup, and vanilla extract and stir until combined. Set aside.

Spiralize the apple using blade 3 (ribbons, see page 7), then place on a serving plate.

Serve the ribbons with the chocolate sauce and chopped nuts on the side. To eat, dip the ribbons in the chocolate and sprinkle over the nuts.

NUTRITION (PER SERVING): 648 calories | 8 g protein | 56 g fat (of which 41 g saturates) | 26 g carbohydrate (of which 23 g sugars) | 4 g fiber | 0.1 g salt

RHUBARB AND APPLE NOODLE CRUMBLE

Preparation time: 10 minutes
Cooking time: 20 minutes

Serves 1

1 medium crisp apple
2 tsp coconut oil, warmed to a liquid
1 strawberry, chopped into small chunks
2 in/5 cm stick rhubarb, chopped into small chunks
1 teaspoon maple syrup
1 tbsp gluten-free oats
1 tbsp unroasted almonds, coarsely chopped

This is a delicious and warming dessert, perfect for the winter months when you want to indulge in something comforting. The rhubarb adds a fragrant punch to the dish and a beautiful pink tinge to the apple noodles. As well as tasting great, rhubarb is also one of the lowest-calorie vegetables out there and, as such, is perfect for weight loss.

Preheat the oven to 400°F/200°C.

Spiralize the apple using blade 2 (medium, see page 7).

Rub 1 teaspoon of the coconut oil around the inside of a small ovenproof ramekin. Place the chopped strawberry and rhubarb in the bottom of the ramekin and drizzle on the maple syrup. Top the rhubarb and strawberry with the noodles and press down to make sure that they are packed in tightly. They will condense and break down during cooking, so don't worry if the ramekin looks overfull.

In a small bowl, combine the oats and almonds and spoon them over the fruit noodles, ensuring that the noodles are completely covered. Drizzle the remaining teaspoon of coconut oil over the crumble and bake in the preheated oven for 20 minutes.

Remove from the oven and allow to cool for 5 minutes before serving.

NUTRITION (PER SERVING): 286 calories | 7 g protein | 16 g fat (of which 6 g saturates) | 27 g carbohydrate (of which 16 g sugars) | 5 g fiber | 0 g salt

HOT NOODLE PUDDING WITH PISTACHIO AND POMEGRANATE

Preparation time: 10 minutes,
plus soaking
Cooking time: 20 minutes

Serves 2

1 large cooking apple

1 tbsp coconut oil, warmed to
a liquid

2 tbsp pistachio nuts, shelled

scant ½ cup/3 oz/85 g
pomegranate seeds

3 tbsp maple syrup

1 cup/4 oz/115 g cashew nuts,
soaked for 2 hours

scant 1 cup/200 ml
coconut milk

3–5 drops of vanilla extract

This dish is a fruity take on a traditional Jewish kugel pudding. Here the egg noodles have been swapped for apple, and the custard is free of dairy and refined sugar, but it remains a rich, creamy, and comforting dessert. This version is studded with pistachio nuts and jewel-like pomegranate seeds, adding little pockets of crunch and bright sparks of sweetness that make it a very special way to end a meal.

Preheat the oven to 325°F/170°C.

Spiralize the apple using blade 3 (ribbon, see page 7), then transfer to a medium baking dish. Pour generous 2 cups/500 ml water over the noodles and set aside for 10 minutes for the noodles to soften.

Strain the noodles, squeezing out as much water as you can with your hands, then return them to the baking dish. Drizzle the coconut oil over the noodles and add the pistachio nuts, pomegranate seeds, and 1 tablespoon of the maple syrup to the dish.

Drain the cashews and place them in a blender along with the coconut milk, vanilla extract, and the remaining maple syrup. Blend until smooth, then pour over the noodles.

Transfer to the oven and bake for 20 minutes until just turning golden at the edges. Allow to cool for 5 minutes before serving.

NUTRITION (PER SERVING): 830 calories | 18 g protein | 60 g fat (of which 26 g saturates) | 50 g carbohydrate (of which 33 g sugars) | 8 g fiber | 0.2 g salt

INDEX

ACKNOWLEDGMENTS

It is a near impossible task to list everyone who has inspired my journey and helped to bring this book together. In the early days of my food explorations my hearty thanks go out to Jason Vale, Kate Beswick, and Kenneth Ryan: my juicy dream team who with relentless passion ignited a flame. To Lyra Culverhouse for having the forethought to "give healthy eating a go," despite years of group Sunday munchies spent watching TV on the sofa. I also give thanks to the inspirational Struan Robertson for introducing me to the charity Love146 who became the focus of the sponsored raw-food fasting that changed my life forever and took me from corporate to kitchen. To the gorgeous Steph McCombes for introducing me to the ever-patient and helpful Daniel Hurst, my editor—hats off to you Dan and the biggest of thanks. Thanks too go to Tracy Sadler, Denisa Rățulea, Aliya Sayakhova, and Heidi Vietz for assisting in the craziest kitchen cook-off ever. And to Sue Whitehead, who in the earliest days of my Explore Raw Cookery School workshops lugged, shopped, carried, and drove my food, me, and my many kitchen machines across London to get me to the kitchen on time.

Lastly I would like to dedicate this book to my family and friends and in particular my brother Kristen (who is a bit gutted that this is going to print before his PhD gets published!), my sister Tracey (who still "oohs" and "aahs" with enthusiastic dedication at every one of my recipes), and to Yousef, who gave me my kitchen.

ABOUT THE AUTHOR

Stephanie Jeffs is a raw food chef and the founder of Explore Raw—a blog that was set up to share recipes that would encourage people to pursue better health by choosing a plant-based, living-foods diet. Her recipes focus on creativity, fun, health, and wellness. She lives in Hertford, England and runs workshops at her cooking school in London. She is the originator of "The Five Foundations of a Raw Food Diet" and "The Six Raw Food Techniques" and infuses these throughout her teaching. Stephanie also runs a range of raw food retreats in Portugal, including Raw Juice Camp, which combines rest, relaxation, and raw fine-dining with fitness and yoga. After leaving a successful international corporate career, Stephanie now focuses her energy as a raw food educator and chef at www.exploreraw.com.

First American edition published in 2015 by

INTERLINK BOOKS
An imprint of Interlink Publishing Group, Inc.
46 Crosby Street
Northampton, Massachusetts 01060
www.interlinkbooks.com

Library of Congress Cataloging-in-Publication Data available

ISBN 978-1-56656-080-1

10 9 8 7 6 5 4 3 2 1

Reproduction by Colourdepth, UK
Printed and bound in Italy

Commissioning editor: Emily Preece-Morrison
Project editor: Daniel Hurst
American edition editor: Leyla Moushabeck
Photographer: Tony Briscoe
Design concept: Laura Russell
Design layout: Rosamund Saunders
Prop stylist: Davina Perkins
Nutritional analyses: Anita Bean
Proofreaders: Wendy Hobson, Jennifer Staltare